CAKEMOJI

RECIPES & IDEAS FOR
SWEET-TALKING TREATS

jenni powell

photography by rita platts

quadrille

PUBLISHING DIRECTOR Sarah Lavelle
COMMISSIONING EDITOR Lisa Pendreigh
EDITORIAL ASSISTANT Harriet Butt
CREATIVE DIRECTOR Helen Lewis
DESIGNERS Katherine Keeble, Vanessa Masci
FOOD STYLIST Marianne Stewart
PHOTOGRAPHER Rita Platts
STYLIST Louie Waller
PRODUCTION DIRECTOR Vincent Smith
PRODUCTION CONTROLLER Jessica Otway

First published in 2016 by
Quadrille Publishing Ltd
Pentagon House
52–54 Southwark Street
London SE1 1UN
www.quadrille.co.uk
www.quadrille.com

Quadrille is an imprint of Hardie Grant
www.hardiegrant.com.au

Reprinted in 2016, 2017
10 9 8 7 6 5 4 3

ISBN 978 1 84949 790 9

introduction 4

EDIBLE EMOJIS
smiley face cakes 6
heart cookies 10
birthday cake 14
cat & dog cakes 18
ghost cake 22
poop cupcakes 26
unicorn cake 30
robot cake 34
pizza slice cake 38
rainbow brownie 42
confetti party popper 44
three wise monkey cake toppers 48
crown mini cakes 52
cake bombs 56
emoji iced cookies 60

BASIC RECIPES AND TECHNIQUES
cake and cookie recipes 68
layering cakes 72
crumbcoating cakes 73
colouring buttercream 74
colouring fondant 75
covering a cake with fondant 76
rolling out cookie dough 79
chocolate ganache 80
royal icing 81

colouring royal icing 82
flooding royal icing 83
making piping bag 84
piping techniques 85

templates 86
#cakemoji 96

INTRODUCTION

Everybody loves emojis. Nowadays, a text message is rarely sent or a post is seldom uploaded without using at least one or two emojis. There is always more than a little excitement online when new emojis are released. So when the lovely people at Quadrille got in touch about creating a cake decorating book based on everyone's favourite little characters, well, I jumped at the chance. Fast forward a good few months of back and forth – comparing our favourite and most-used emojis to decide those we wanted to include, discussing the cakes we wanted to create and, most importantly, how to combine the two – and *Cakemoji* is finally here.

As well as speaking emoji, let's start eating emoji too. *Cakemoji* is a collection of different emoji-themed bakes that we hope everyone will enjoy making and sharing. We've based the projects around some of our favourite emojis, but once you've learned the various techniques you can apply them to any emoji you fancy.

The cakes themselves are all super simple yet delicious recipes that I'm sure you'll be baking over and over. (Try the brownie recipe, still warm and gooey from the oven, with a dollop of ice cream and some caramel sauce – you can thank me later.)

I have a very relaxed approach to cake decorating, and I hope that rubs off on you a little. Making cakes is fun, so take your time with the steps and don't worry if things don't go the way you expect straight away – it will still look and taste amazing.

DIFFICULTY LEVELS

beginners

intermediate

expert

We mention a few pieces of specialist equipment throughout this book,but there are often other options you can use that will work just as well, which you probably already have in the kitchen.

Don't forget to take a picture of your emoji cakes and share them online with the hashtag #cakemoji. We can't wait to see what you make.

SMILEY FACE CAKES

YOU WILL NEED

Three 15cm (6 in.) round sponges
in the flavour of your choice, made
following the recipe on page 68

One quantity of filling in the
flavour of your choice (see page 70)

One quantity of buttercream
in the flavour of your choice
(see page 70)

740g (26 oz.) yellow fondant, either
pre-coloured or coloured following
the instructions on page 80

Small amount of fondant
in each of the colours needed
to make the facial features,
black, white, red, blue, pink

Edible glue and paintbrush

Paper template of your chosen emoji
(see pages 86–7 and opposite)

DIFFICULTY

1. Level and layer the sponges, following the instructions on pages 72–74 using the filling of your choice.

2. Crumbcoat the sponges with a thin layer of buttercream, following the instructions on pages 76–77. Chill for 30 minutes in the fridge.

3. Roll out the yellow fondant on a lightly dusted worksurface to 5mm (⅛ in.) thickness, preferably using spacers to ensure an even thickness.

4. Carefully lift up the rolled-out fondant and use it to cover the layered sponges, following the instructions on pages 82–83.

5. Roll out the coloured fondants to 3mm (⅛ in.) thickness. Using paper templates and a sharp knife, cut out the facial details as necessary.

6. Check the fondant facial features are in the correct configuration. Using edible glue, stick the white teeth in position on the black mouth.

FOR THE CRYING-LAUGHING FACE EMOJI: cut eyes, eyebrows, and mouth from black fondant; cut teeth from white fondant; cut tears from blue fondant.

FOR THE KISSY FACE EMOJI: cut eyes, eyebrows, and mouth from black fondant; cut heart from red fondant.

FOR THE COOL DUDE FACE EMOJI: cut sunglasses and mouth from black fondant.

7. Beginning with the mouth, place each fondant facial feature on to the cake top. Refer to the emoji to make sure each piece is in its exact position.

8. Once you are happy with the position of each fondant facial feature, using edible glue, stick the pieces on to the cake top.

TO MAKE A PAPER TEMPLATE: On pages 86–87 you will find a full-size template for the crying-laughing face and half-size templates for the kissy face and cool dude face to enlarge.

For any other emoji, do an internet search then download and enlarge the emoji until it is 15cm (6 in.) in diameter. To make a bigger cake, enlarge the emoji until the diameter of the face matches the size of the cake. Using this enlargement, trace off each separate facial feature – eyes, eyebrows, mouth, kiss, sunglasses – and cut them out from paper.

HEART COOKIES

YOU WILL NEED

For the heart cookies:

One quantity of cookie dough, made following the recipe on page 70

85g (3 oz./½ cup) rainbow sugar sprinkles (bright as possible, so the colours withstand the oven temperature)

Half quantity of royal icing (see page 81), divided and coloured with red, yellow, blue, green, and purple, plus white colours to match the heart emojis

Small amount of yellow fondant

Edible pearl lustre and gold sprays

For the love letter cookies:

One quantity cookie dough, made following the recipe on page 70

250g (9 oz.) white fondant

Small amount of red fondant

DIFFICULTY

1. Make a quantity of cookie dough. Add the sugar sprinkles to the dough and chill for 30 minutes. Roll out the dough. Using a 10cm (4 in.) heart cutter, cut out heart-shaped cookies.

2. Transfer the heart-shaped cookies to baking trays lined with baking parchment. Bake in a preheated oven at 180°C/350°F/gas mark 6 following the instructions on page 79.

3. Once the cookies are completely cool, decorate with icing. Following the instructions on pages 80–85, make and fill a piping bag with your chosen colour royal icing. Pipe the heart outline around the cookie edge.

4. Following the instructions on page 83, thin the same colour royal icing down to flooding consistency and use it to flood inside the heart outline. To remove any air bubbles, tap the cookies flat on the worksurface.

5. Using stiff peak white icing, pipe an arch at the top of the heart, on both sides, to create the highlights.

6. Using a scriber tool or toothpick, drag the white icing at the edges so it bleeds into the coloured icing to create a softer line. Allow to dry for 3-4 hours, preferably overnight.

7. Roll out the yellow fondant to 2mm (¹⁄₁₆ in.) thickness. Using a 3cm (1¼ in.) round cutter, cut out two yellow fondant dics. Using just the edge of the cutter, take away slivers of the disc to create the starbust shape.

TIP:
Once you have cut out your fondant starburst shapes, leave them for 30 minutes to allow the fondant to firm up. This makes the fondant shapes easier to handle.

8. Spray each of the starburst shapes with edible metallic gold lustre.

9. Once the cookie is dry, spray lightly with edible pearl lustre. Using a dab of royal icing, fix the starburst shapes to the cookie, placing one at the top right and one at the bottom left.

1. Make a quantity of cookie dough and chill it for 30 minutes. Roll out the dough and cut into rectangles 10cm (4 in.) by 6.5cm (2½ in.). Bake following the instructions on page 79.

2. Roll out the red fondant to 3mm (⅛ in.) thickness. Using a 2.5m (1 in.) heart cutter, cut out the same number of tiny red fondant hearts as you have baked cookies.

3. Once the cookies are cool, roll out the white fondant to 3mm (⅛ in.) thickness. Using one of the cookies as a template, cut fondant rectangles to the exact size of the cookies.

4. Using a little royal icing or edible glue, adhere the fondant rectangles to the cookies. Using a cake smoother, work across the fondant to create a perfectly smooth surface.

5. Using a sharp knife, score lines in the top of the white fondant from each corner diagonally inwards to create the envelope flaps.

6. Using a tiny dab of royal icing, fix the red fondant heart to the envelope cookie, placing the heart at the point where the scored lines on the envelope meet.

BIRTHDAY
CAKE

Three 20cm (8 in.) round sponges, in the flavour of your choice, made following the recipe on page 68

One quantity of filling in the flavour of your choice (see page 70)

One quantity of buttercream in the flavour of your choice (see page 70)

1kg (2 lb.) white fondant

250g (9 oz.) red fondant, either pre-coloured or coloured following the instructions on page 80

500g (1 lb.) white florist paste

Small amount of yellow fondant

Edible glue and paintbrush

Cakepop sticks

DIFFICULTY

1. Level and layer the sponges, following the instructions on pages 72–74 using the filling of your choice.

2. Crumbcoat the sponges with a thin layer of buttercream, following the instructions on pages 76–77. Chill for 30 minutes in the fridge.

3. Roll out the white fondant on a lightly dusted worksurface to 3mm (1/8 in.) thickness, preferably using spacers to ensure an even thickness.

4. Carefully lift up the rolled-out fondant and use it to cover the layered sponges, following the instructions on pages 82–83.

5. To make the raspberries, divide the red fondant into eight even-sized pieces. Roll each piece into a neat ball.

6. Shape each ball into a raspberry by rolling it between your palms to make a slightly pointed top. Tap each raspberry on your worksurface to flatten the base.

7. Using a ball tool or the rounded end of a paintbrush, make divots all over each of the raspberries.

TIP:
When handling white or pale coloured fondant, make sure you wear pale clothing with no fuzzy fibres.

8. To make the candles, divide the white florist paste into three even-sized pieces.

9. Using cake smoothers to keep the white florist paste clean, roll each of the three pieces into a thick candle and neaten up the ends.

10. Brush the cakepop sticks with edible glue and carefully push one down through the centre of each candle.

11. Using cake smoothers, work each candle between the smoothers to lengthen it and give a neat finish. Cut down the cakepop stick so that only 1cm (⅜ in.) is visible.

12. To make the flames, divide the yellow fondant into three even-sized pieces. Roll each piece into a neat ball, then shape it into a flame by elongating the top into a point.

13. Dab a small amount of edible glue onto the top of each cakepop stick, then carefully push a yellow flame onto the top of each stick.

14. Using royal icing, position the three candles on the cake top, equally spacing the candles in a line across the centre.

15. Using royal icing, position the raspberries on the cake top, equally spacing the raspberries around the outside edge with four on each side of the line of candles.

CAT & DOG CAKES

YOU WILL NEED

Three 20cm (8 in.) round sponges, in the flavour of your choice, made following the recipe on page 68, per cat or dog cake

One quantity of filling in the flavour of your choice (see page 70)

One quantity of buttercream in the flavour of your choice (see page 70)

For the cat cake: 740g (26 oz.) yellow fondant, either pre-coloured or coloured following the instructions on page 80
For the dog cake: 740g (26 oz.) white fondant

Small amounts of fondant in each of the colours needed to make the facial features
For the cat: tan, pink, black and white
For the dog: brown, black, pink and white

Edible glue and paintbrush

Paper templates (see pages 88–9)

DIFFICULTY

1. Level and layer the sponges, following the instructions on pages 72–74 using the filling of your choice.

2. Place the template on the cake top and, using a sharp knife, cut around the edge through all the layers. Remove any excess pieces and neaten the sides if necessary.

3. Crumbcoat the sponges with a thin layer of buttercream, following the instructions on pages 76–77, using a small palette knife to work around the shaped edges. Chill for 30 minutes in the fridge.

4. Roll out the yellow or white fondant on a lightly dusted work-surface to 3mm (⅛ in.) thickness and use it to cover the shaped sponges, following the instructions on pages 82–83.

TO MAKE A PAPER TEMPLATE:
On pages 88–89 you will find full-size templates for the cat and dog faces. If you want to make the panda, pig, lion, or any other favourite animal face then do an internet search for that emoji. Download and enlarge the emoji until it is 20cm (8 in.) in diameter. To make a bigger cake, enlarge the emoji until the diameter of the face matches the size of the cake. Using this enlargement, trace off each separate facial feature – eyes, nose, mouth – and cut them out from paper.

5. Using cake smoothers for the cake top and your hands for the sides, mould the fondant to the shaped cake. Trim away the excess fondant from the base of the cake.

6. Roll out the coloured fondants to 3mm (⅛ in.) thickness. Using paper templates and a sharp knife, cut out the facial features as necessary. For the cat, cut eyes, nose, mouth, and ear pieces.

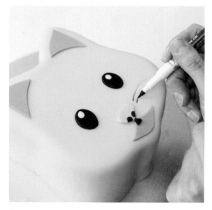

7. Using edible glue, stick the facial features to the cake top. Refer to the emoji to make sure each piece is in the right place and layers are in the correct order. For the cat, start with the brown ears and mouth.

8. Add the white pupils to the black eyes before positioning them on the cake top – it is easier to make adjustments off the cake. If preferred, add two small black nostrils to the pink nose for more definition.

9. For fine details such as the cat's whiskers, using edible black pen, draw on fine lines either side of the pink nose across the cat's cheeks.

GHOST CAKE

YOU WILL NEED

Two 20cm (8 in.) square chocolate sponges, made following the recipe on page 68

One quantity of filling in the flavour of your choice (see page 70)

One quantity of buttercream in the flavour of your choice (see page 70)

Small amounts of fondant in each of the colours needed to make the facial features: black, white and pink

Small liquorice sweet

Oreo cookie

Paper template (see page 90)

DIFFICULTY

1. Level and layer the sponges, following the instructions on pages 72–74 using the filling of your choice. Place the paper template for the body on the cake top and, using a sharp knife, cut around the edge.

2. Take the largest cake offcuts and place the arm templates on top. In the same way, cutting through all the sponge layers, cut around the edge of the templates to give one left arm and one right arm.

3. Position the arms in the correct place using the paper template as a guide.

4. Remove the paper templates and then, using some buttercream, stick the arms in position on the body.

TIPS:
If tight on time, buttercream can be made a few days in advance and stored in the refrigerator. Before using, allow the buttercream to come back to room temperature and beat well.

Keep the buttercream you use for crumbcoating the cake separate from the buttercream you use for the final layer, this is to avoid visible cake crumbs in the finished cake. You can add a tiny amount of violet food colouring to the buttercream to counteract any yellowness.

5. Crumbcoat the sponges with a thin layer of buttercream, following the instructions on pages 76–77, using a small palette knife to work around the shaped cake. Chill for 30 minutes in the fridge.

6. Using a small palette knife, cover the top and sides of the cake with a fresh quantity of buttercream.

7. Roll out the coloured fondants to 3mm (⅛ in.) thickness. Using your templates and a sharp knife, cut out the facial features. For the eyes and mouth, cut from black fondant. For the tongue, cut from pink fondant.

8. Place the blade of a sharp knife vertically along the centre of the pink fondant tongue. Lightly score a line, but be careful not to cut all the way through the fondant.

9. Place the black fondant mouth on the cake top, pushing it slightly into the buttercream. Then add the pink fondant tongue on top of the mouth. Refer to the emoji to make sure each piece is in the right place.

10. Place the small liquorice sweet in the correct position for the right eye. Finally, place the large Oreo cookie in the exact position for the larger left eye.

POOP
CUPCAKES

YOU WILL NEED

12 chocolate cupcakes, made
following the recipe on page 70

One quantity chocolate buttercream
(see page 70)

Small amounts of fondant in each
of the colours needed to make
the facial features: black and white

Edible glue and paintbrush

Paper template (see page 90)

1. Roll out the white and black fondants
on a lightly dusted worksurface
to 3mm (⅛ in.) thickness, preferably
using spacers to ensure an even
thickness.

2. Using the paper templates and
a sharp knife or small oval and
round cutters, cut out 24 eyes and
12 mouths from white fondant,
then 24 pupils from black fondant.

3. Using edible glue, stick the black
pupils centrally on top of the white
eyes. Once you have cut out your
fondant shapes, leave them to dry for
2–3 hours so they are easier to handle.

4. Fit a large open nozzle in a
piping bag and fill with chocolate
buttercream. Before serving, pipe
buttercream swirls on each cupcake.

DIFFICULTY

6. Carefully position two eyes and one mouth on each cupcake, pressing the fondant features gently into the buttercream piping.

5. When piping, use smooth circular motions and lift off the nozzle upwards as you complete the swirl. This ensures perky poops.

7. Don't forget to photograph your poop cupcakes and share them with the hashtag #cakemoji.

UNICORN CAKE

YOU WILL NEED

One quantity of 20cm (8 in.) round sponge cake batter, in the flavour of your choice, made following the recipe on page 68, then divided into five equal parts with each fifth being coloured with either pink, purple, blue, green, or yellow gel food colouring

One quantity of filling in the flavour of your choice (see page 70)

One quantity of buttercream in the flavour of your choice (see page 70)

Small amounts of fondant in the following colours, white, black, yellow, green, blue, pink, red

Edible glue and paintbrush

Edible dust in pink and purple

Edible gold stars and sugar balls

Paper template (see page 92)

DIFFICULTY

1. Bake, cool, then level and layer the sponges, following the instructions on pages 72–74 using the filling of your choice, placing the layers in the following order – yellow, green, blue, purple, and red.

2. Crumbcoat the layered sponges with a thin layer of buttercream, following the instructions on pages 76–77. Chill for 30 minutes in the refrigerator.

3. Divide the remaining buttercream into four equal parts. Colour three of the quarters with blue, purple, or pink gel food colouring. Add green food colouring to a tiny bit of the fourth buttercream. Place in piping bags.

4. Pipe generous stripes of coloured buttercream around the sides of the cake. Start with the blue buttercream, covering the bottom third of the sides. Repeat with the purple buttercream in the centre and finish with the pink.

5. Pipe the remaining pink buttercream around the cake top. Using a palette knife, smooth the buttercream surface.

6. Using a metal scraper, work around the sides of the cake to smooth and blend the coloured stripes together. For smoother buttercream, warm the scraper by placing it under a hot tap.

7. Using a palette knife, level up the buttercream surface on the cake top again, removing any excess.

8. Roll out the white and coloured fondants to 3mm (⅛ in.) thickness. Using your paper templates and a sharp knife, carefully cut out the main head shape from white fondant.

9. Using a knife and small cutters, cut out the facial features from the coloured fondants. Use pink for inner ears, purple for snout and mane, black for eye and nostril, white for pupil, and bright colours for the horn.

10. Brush the snout and mane pieces with pink and purple edible dusts, blending the colours together to add shade and highlights.

11. Using edible glue, stick the facial features to the unicorn head. Refer to the emoji to make sure each piece is in the right place.

12. To add some shading to the unicorn, use edible dusts in pink and purple. Using a dry, soft paintbrush, pick up a small amount of edible dust and work gently, slowly building up the layers of colour.

13. Using pink buttercream to hold it in place, carefully position your fondant unicorn on the cake top.

14. Starting with the largest nozzle size, pipe swirls around one edge of the cake then build up the design, finishing with the smallest nozzles.

15. Pipe stars and dots down the sides of the cake in the different colours of buttercream.

16. Finish off the cake with additional sprinkles, such as edible gold sugar balls and glittery gold stars.

ROBOT CAKE

YOU WILL NEED

Two 20cm (8 in.) square sponges, in the flavour of your choice, made following the recipe on page 68

One quantity of filling in the flavour of your choice (see page 70)

One quantity of buttercream in the flavour of your choice (see page 70)

1kg (2 lb.) blue-grey fondant, either pre-coloured or coloured following the instructions on page 80

Small amounts of fondant in each colour needed for the facial features: white, royal blue, red, and black

Edible dust in bluegrass

Edible metallic pale blue lustre spray

Liquorice catherine wheel

Lollipop sprayed gold

Two red fruit roll-ups

Two white sweets

Paper template (see page 92)

DIFFICULTY

1. Level and layer the sponges, following the instructions on pages 72–74. Crumbcoat the sponges with a thin layer of buttercream, following the instructions on pages 76–77. Chill for 30 minutes in the refrigerator.

2. Roll out the blue-grey fondant to 3mm (⅛ in.) thickness, preferably using spacers to ensure an even thickness. Cover the cake with the rolled-out fondant, following the instructions on pages 82–83.

3. Prepare the coloured dust on a paper towel by blending the bluegrass edible dust gradually with cornflour to achieve a lighter shade.

4. Apply the dust to the cake top and sides, working with a lighter shade to start with and gradually building up the colour strength a little at a time.

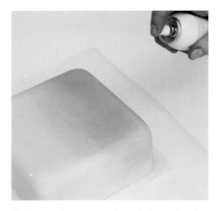

5. Spray the covered and dusted cake with edible metallic lustre.

6. Roll out the coloured fondants to 2mm (¹⁄₁₆ in.) thickness. Using a 2.5cm (1 in.) round cutter, cut out two blue circles for the eyes.

7. Using the paper templates and a sharp knife, cut out the row of teeth from white fondant, the nose from red fondant and the mouth from black fondant.

8. Mark the position of each of the facial features lightly on to the fondant cake top to make sure they are positioned correctly.

9. Following the markings, place the blue eyes, red nose and black mouth in position on the cake top. Add the white sweet eyes on top.

TIP:
You can use the same techniques explained here to recreate any other emoji that you fancy. As well as cutting out facial features from rolled-out fondant, look for fun and colourful sweets and candy that can be used for eyes, ears, or mouths.

11. Using a tiny blob of fondant to hold it in place, push the lollipop stick all the way into the cake through the centre of the liquorice wheel so only the gold lollipop can be seen.

10. Using royal icing, stick the liquorice catherine wheel to the top of the head, curving it over the edge of the cake top and down to the side edge.

12. Using royal icing, stick one red fruit roll-up on each side of the cake for the ears.

PIZZA SLICE CAKE

YOU WILL NEED

25cm (10 in.) round vanilla sponge, made following the recipe on page 68

One quantity of buttercream in the flavour of your choice (see page 70)

740g (26 oz.) ivory fondant

Red food colouring

100g (3½ oz./⅓ cup) raspberry jam

Small amount of deep red fondant

DIFFICULTY

1. Once the sponge is cool, place a 20cm (8 in.) cake board or plate on top and score around the edge. Scoop out some of the top layer of sponge to create a raised 'pizza crust'.

2. Coat the entire cake with a thin layer of buttercream.

3. For the crust, roll out the ivory fondant into a sausage wide enough to cover the cake's outer edge. Do not make it smooth – keep it uneven, like a pizza crust.

4. Cover the 'crust' with the fondant sausage, taking the fondant over the inside edge of the 'crust'.

5. Using a kitchen blow torch on a medium setting, toast the fondant crust to build up the colour. Keep the torch moving to avoid burnt patches.

6. For the sauce, add a few drops of red food colouring to the remaining buttercream, then mix through the raspberry jam. Spread the sauce over the centre of the cake, up to the crust.

7. For the pepperoni slices, roll out and cut 2.5–3cm (1– 1¼ in.) discs from the red fondant. Using a ball tool or rounded end of a brush, make divots.

8. For the 'cheese', melt the white chocolate in a microwave and pour it over the centre of the cake to cover the 'sauce'. Leave to set.

9. Using a kitchen blow torch on a medium setting, toast the chocolate to add colour. Keep the torch moving. Scatter the 'pepperoni slices' across the centre of the pizza.

TIP:
To replicate the pizza emoji exactly, visually divide the entire pizza into eighths and then place five slices of fondant pepperoni on each eighth slice of the cake.

RAINBOW BROWNIES

23cm (9 in.) square brownie cake, made following the recipe on page 69

Half quantity of buttercream in the flavour of your choice (see page 70)

Selection of small candies and confectionery, such as Nerds, Skittles, and TicTacs, in the colours of the rainbow – red, orange, yellow, green, blue, and purple

1. Once the brownie is completely cool, remove from the tin. Using a large sharp knife, trim the brownie into a perfect square.

2. Coat the brownie with a thin layer of buttercream, following the instructions on page 73. Chill the cake for 30 minutes in the refrigerator.

3. Place three rows of white candies around the outside edge of the cake top to create a square border. Starting with the green candies, place them in an arch from the bottom left corner to the top right corner.

4. Repeat with the other colour candies, to complete the rainbow. Once the rainbow is in place, fill the remaining gaps with blue candies.

DIFFICULTY

CONFETTI
PARTY
POPPER

Waffle cones

Selection of confectionery

One quantity of buttercream in the flavour of your choice (see page 70)

170g (6 oz.) yellow fondant per confetti cone, either pre-coloured or coloured following the instructions on page 80

Small amounts of blue, red, orange, and yellow fondant, either pre-coloured or coloured following the instructions on page 80

Edible glue and paintbrush

Edible metallic gold lustre spray

DIFFICULTY

1. Place your chosen selection of confectionery in a bowl and mix them together. Fill each of the waffle cones with a handful of mixed candies until about two thirds full.

2. Roll out the yellow fondant to 3mm (1/8 in.) thickness. Using a round cutter the same diameter as the open end of the cone, cut out a fondant disc.

3. Using a small palette knife, fill the end of the cone with buttercream to seal in the candies. Spread a small amount of buttercream around the top outside edge of the cone.

4. Place the yellow fondant disc over the open end of the cone filled with buttercream and press down to seal. Place the cone in a glass and leave to set for 30 minutes.

5. Using a small palette knife, coat the outsides of the waffle cone with a thin layer of buttercream.

6. Place the coated cone onto the rolled out yellow fondant, laying the cone on its side.

7. Wrap the cone in the yellow fondant by rolling it until the edges of the fondant meet. Trim away any excess fondant to give a neat finish.

8. Using a smaller round cutter, cut another yellow fondant disc to the same size as the recessed end of the covered cone.

9. Using edible glue, stick the small yellow fondant disc in place at the wide end of the covered cone to give a neat finish.

10. Spray the fondant-covered cone with edible metallic gold lustre spray.

11. For the confetti, roll out the coloured fondants to 2mm (¹⁄₁₆ in.) thickness. Using a sharp knife, cut out long thin strips. Using a small square cutter, punch out small squares. To assemble the confetti cone, lay the cone down on its side, then drape the long thin strips of fondant to make the confetti streamers and scatter the small fondant squares around.

THREE WISE MONKEY CAKE TOPPERS

---------- YOU WILL NEED ----------

Chocolate mini sponge cakes, made following the recipe on page 69

One quantity of chocolate buttercream (see page 70)

One quantity of buttercream in the flavour of your choice (see page 70), divided and coloured into three different shades

200g (7 oz.) brown florist paste

Small amounts of fondant in each colour needed for the facial features: dark brown, light brown, black, white, and red

Toothpicks

Edible glue and paintbrush

Paper template (see page 91)

---------- DIFFICULTY ----------

1. Lightly dust the worksurface with cornflour to prevent any sticking, then roll out the brown florist paste to 5mm (¼ in.) thickness, preferably using spacers to ensure an even thickness.

2. Using the templates and a sharp knife, cut out the monkey heads from brown florist paste. For the toppers to stand upright, you need to use florist paste. Otherwise, you can use fondant.

3. Working quickly, while the florist paste is still soft, insert two toothpicks into the base of each monkey head. Push the toothpicks half way into the monkey heads, making sure the toothpicks do not poke out the paste.

4. Roll out the coloured fondants to 3mm (⅛ in.) thickness. Using your paper templates and a sharp knife, carefully cut out the facial details from the different coloured fondants as necessary.

5. Using edible glue and a paintbrush, stick the fondant facial features in place on top of the florist paste monkey shape. Leave to dry overnight.

6. Bake mini chocolate sponge cakes or chocolate cupcakes, following the instructions on pages 69–70. For mini cakes, level the sponges and cut out circles using round cutters the same width as the monkey heads.

7. Layer the mini chocolate sponge cakes, following the instructions on page 72 using chocolate buttercream or the filling of your choice.

TIP:
Florist paste starts to set very quickly so you need to work fast when handling it. However, the florist paste needs to be left to dry overnight in order to be completely set and hold its shape when stood up.

8. Place the coloured buttercream into a piping bag and pipe swirls on top of each mini cake or cupcake.

9. To position the monkey cake topper on the cake, insert the toothpicks into the centre top of each cake until stable.

CROWN MINI CAKES

20cm (8 in.) square vanilla sponge cake (see page 68)

One quantity of filling of your choice (see page 70)

One quantity of buttercream of your choice (see page 70)

200g (7 oz.) golden yellow fondant mixed with 100g (3½ oz.) florist paste

Small amount of pink fondant or candies for the 'jewels'

Edible glue and paintbrush

Edible metallic gold lustre spray

Paper template (see page 91)

TIP:
For the crown, use two parts fondant mixed with one part florist paste for extra strength.

DIFFICULTY

1. Bake a 20cm (8 in.) square sponge, following the recipe on page 68. Cut out rounds of sponge using an 8cm (3 in.) round cutter.

2. Level and layer the sponges, following the instructions on page 72 using the filling of your choice.

3. Crumbcoat the layered cake with a thin layer of buttercream, following the instructions on page 73. Chill for 30 minutes in the refrigerator.

4. Lightly dust the worksurface with cornflour to prevent sticking, then roll out the golden yellow fondant to 3mm (⅛ in.) thickness, preferably using spacers to ensure an even thickness.

5. Using the same 8cm (3 in.) round cutter, cut out a disc from the rolled-out golden yellow fondant and place on the cake top.

6. Using the paper template and a sharp knife, carefully cut out the crown shape from the rolled-out golden yellow fondant.

7. Using either cut-out pink fondant oval shapes or small candies, add the jewels to the crown referring to the template for positioning.

8. Using edible glue and a paintbrush, wrap the fondant crown around each mini cake and glue the overlapping ends in place.

9. With the same 8cm (3 in.) round cutter in place to hold up the fondant crown, spray the covered cake with edible metallic gold lustre.

TO MAKE A PAPER TEMPLATE:
On page 91 you will find a half-size template for the crown to enlarge. Photocopy the template at 200% and then cut it out from paper. To cover an 8cm (3 in.) diameter cake, the fondant crown needs to be 23cm (9 in.) long.

TIP:
Leave the cookie cutter in place for a few hours while you leave the fondant crown to firm up. Take care when removing the cutter as, even when fully dry, the fondant will still be very fragile.

CAKE BOMBS

YOU WILL NEED

170g (6 oz.) chocolate sponge offcuts, left over from the Ghost Cake or Three Wise Monkey Mini Cakes

85g (3 oz.) popping candy

100g (3½ oz.) chocolate ganache (see page 80)

150g (5½ oz.) dark chocolate, melted for dipping

Edible black lustre spray

Small amount of black fondant

Indoor sparklers

DIFFICULTY

1. Crumble into a bowl the cake offcuts from another recipe, such as the Ghost Cake or Three Wise Monkey Mini Cakes.

2. Add a spoonful of ganache to the cake crumbs and, using your hands, combine until you can mould the mixture with your hands into a ball.

3. Add the popping candy to the mixture and give a final mix (it may be easier to use your hands at this stage).

4. Take some of the mixture and roll it into a ball with your hands. Repeat with the rest of the cake mix. Place the balls on a baking tray and chill for 30 minutes in the fridge.

5. Melt the dark chocolate in a microwave or a heatproof bowl over a saucepan of simmering water. Dip the cakepop sticks into the chocolate and insert one into each cake ball.

6. Put them back into the fridge for a few minutes to set. Dip the cake balls into the melted chocolate and let any excess drip off. Place the sticks into a cake dummy to let the chocolate set.

7. Spray each cake ball with edible metallic black lustre spray. Insert the sticks back into the cake dummy to let the coatings dry.

8. Once dry, carefully remove the sticks from the cake balls, taking care not to dent or crack the dark chocolate coating.

9. For the bomb's fuse, roll a small piece of black fondant in a long sausage and cut into rounds. Pipe ganache into the hole left by the stick then cover with the fondant fuse.

10. When ready to serve, insert an indoor sparkler into the black fondant and light.

EMOJI ICED COOKIES

Makes approximately 12–16 cookies, depending on their size

Two quantities of basic cookie dough (see page 71)

One quantity of royal icing (see page 81)

Paste food colours in as many colours as necessary for your chosen emoji

Paper templates (see pages 94–5)

DIFFICULTY

1. Preheat the oven to 175°C/350°F/ gas mark 4. Line two baking trays with parchment. Make a double quantity of cookie dough, following the recipe on page 71. Chill in the fridge. Roll out the dough to 5mm (¼ in.) thickness.

3. List all the emojis you are making in cookie form and the colours you need to ice each design. For the nerd emoji face cookie we used bright yellow, light brown, black and white royal icing.

2. Using a cookie cutter or templates and a sharp knife, cut out cookie shapes following the instructions on page 79. Transfer to the prepared trays and bake following the instructions on page 71. Leave to cool completely.

TIP:
When icing cookies you need two different consistencies of royal icing. Soft-peak or outline icing, which is thick enough to create outlines and boundaries that stop different coloured icings from mixing together, and flooding icing, which is runnier and quickly fills in large areas. The soft-peak icing is also used to add extra details on top after the flooding icing has dried.

TIPS:
Colour up 2–3 tablespoons of icing for each colour required for your chosen emojis. For shades that you will use more of – such as the emoji face yellow – then colour up a few extra tablespoons of icing.

When icing cookies, always outline and flood one colour at a time. Allow the icing to dry completely before adding the next colour to the cookie. This prevents the colours from bleeding into each other.

4. Make up a quantity of soft-peak/outline royal icing following the instructions on page 81. This will be enough to ice 12–16 cookies. Depending on your chosen emojis, colour up the amounts that you need.

5. List all the different shades you require to ice your chosen emojis. Using a toothpick, add tiny amounts of your chosen gel food colour to a small amount of icing and mix until it matches the emoji colour.

6. Make a paper piping bag, fitting the bag with a 1.5 plain nozzle. Using a palette knife, place the soft-peak icing into the piping bag (see pages 84–85).

7. Referring to the instructions on page 85 on how to hold the piping bag and pipe the outlines, carefully follow all the lines that need to be piped in that outline colour.

8. For the nerd emoji face cookie, we piped the face, eyes and mouth outlines in bright yellow.

10. Fill the outlined area with the flooding icing in the same colour. If necessary, gently tap the cookie to help the icing fill the entire area. Do not overfill the area or the icing will overflow the outlines.

9. Once the outlines in that colour are piped, place some of the icing back in the bowl and, following the instructions on page 83, thin it with water until a flooding consistency. Place the flooding icing in a fresh piping bag and snip off a tiny piece at the tip of the bag.

11. Repeat with each colour needed to complete the emoji design. Allow the icing to dry completely before adding an extra details.

12. To add any surface details, such as the glasses and teeth, using soft-peak icing, carefully pipe any extra lines, dots or other shapes on top of the dry iced cookie.

TIP:
To make it look like someone has taken a bite out of the cookie, pipe some bite marks within the outline on one side of the cookie before flooding in the centre.

1. For the sushi cookie, or any other cookie where you want the icing colours to blend, pipe the outline in soft-peak icing as usual.

2. Flood the outline with the same white icing thinned down to flooding consistency.

3. While the white flooding icing is still wet, pipe a swirl of additional pink icing for the filling of the sushi roll.

4. Tap the cookie on a hard surface to remove any air bubbles and help the two colours to sink into each other.

1. For the donut cookie, pipe the outline for the first colour – pale brown – then flood the area. Allow it to dry before piping the outline for the second colour – dark brown.

2. Flood the second colour – dark brown, taking care to stay within the piped outlines.

3. Scatter over some sugar sprinkles immediately whilst the icing is still wet.

15CM (6 IN.) VANILLA CAKE

for emoji face cakes

YOU WILL NEED

250g (9 oz./1 cup + 2 tbsp)
unsalted butter, softened

250g (9 oz./1¼ cups)
caster (granulated) sugar

5 eggs

1 tsp vanilla bean paste

250g (9 oz./2 cups)
self-raising (self-rising) flour, sifted

1. Line three 15cm (6 in.) tins with greaseproof paper.
2. Preheat the oven to 160°C/325°F/ gas mark 3.
3. Beat the butter in a mixer until it is soft then add the sugar and beat until the mixture is light and pale.
4. Add the eggs and vanilla paste, then mix again.
5. Add the flour and mix gently until everything is just combined.
6. Divide the cake batter between the prepared tins and bake for 25–30 minutes.
7. To test the cakes are ready, insert a toothpick. If it comes out clean, they are cooked. If not ready, return to the oven for a few more minutes.
8. Turn out onto wire racks to cool.

20CM (8 IN.) VANILLA CAKE

for cat & dog cakes and birthday cake

YOU WILL NEED

350g (12⅓ oz./1½ cups + 2 tsp)
unsalted butter, softened

350g (12⅓ oz./1¾ cups)
caster (granulated) sugar

7 eggs

1½ tsp vanilla bean paste

350g (12⅓ oz./2⅔ cups)
self-raising (self-rising) flour, sifted

1. Line three 20cm (8 in.) tins with greaseproof paper.
2. Preheat the oven to 160°C/325°F/ gas mark 3.
3. Beat the butter in a mixer until it is soft then add the sugar and beat until the mixture is light and pale.
4. Add the eggs and vanilla paste, then mix again.
5. Add the flour and mix gently until everything is just combined.
6. Divide the cake batter between the prepared tins and bake for 30–35 minutes.
7. To test the cakes are ready, insert a toothpick. If it comes out clean, they are cooked. If not ready, return to the oven for a few more minutes.
8. Turn out onto wire racks to cool.

25CM (10 IN.) VANILLA CAKE

for pizza cake and unicorn cake

YOU WILL NEED

450g (1 lb./2 cups)
unsalted butter, softened

450g (1 lb./2¼ cups)
caster (granulated) sugar

9 eggs

2 tsp vanilla bean paste

450g (1 lb./scant 3½ cups)
self-raising (self-rising) flour, sifted

1. Line one 25cm (10 in.) tin for the pizza or line five 20cm (8 in.) tins for the unicorn with greaseproof paper.
2. Preheat the oven to 160°C/325°F/ gas mark 3.
3. Beat the butter in a mixer until it is soft then add the sugar and beat until the mixture is light and pale.
4. Add the eggs and vanilla paste, then mix again.
5. Add the flour and mix gently until everything is just combined.
6. For the pizza, pour the cake batter into the prepared tin and bake for 50–55 minutes. For the unicorn, divide the cake batter into five bowls and colour each one (see page 30). Pour each coloured batter into a tin and bake for 30–35 minutes.
8. Turn out onto wire racks to cool.

CHOCOLATE CAKE

for three wise monkey mini cakes with cake leftover for cake bombs

YOU WILL NEED

300g (10½ oz./1⅓ cups) unsalted butter, softened

500g (18 oz./2½ cups) caster (granulated) sugar

8 eggs

680ml (23 fl. oz./2¾ cups + 2 tbsp) milk

400g (14 oz./3 cups) self-raising (self-rising) flour, sifted

4 tsp baking powder

4 tsp instant coffee granules

280g (10 oz./3 cups) cocoa powder, unsweetened

1. Line three 20cm (8 in.) tins with baking parchment.
2. Preheat the oven to 160°C/325°F/gas mark 3.
3. Make the batter following the method given for the chocolate cupcakes on page 70.
4. Divide the batter between the tins and bake for 30–35 minutes.
5. To test the cakes are ready, insert a toothpick. If it comes out clean, they are cooked. If not ready, return to the oven for a few more minutes.
8. Turn out onto wire racks to cool.

CHOCOLATE BROWNIE

for rainbow brownie

YOU WILL NEED

300g (10½ oz./2 cups) dark chocolate chips

150g (5⅓ oz./⅔ cup) unsalted butter, softened

2 tsp ground coffee

325g (11½ oz./1½ cups + 2 tbsp) caster (granulated) sugar

125g (4½ oz./1 cup) plain (all-purpose) flour, sifted

3 eggs, beaten

cocoa powder for dusting

1. Prepare one 20cm (8 in.) square tin by greasing it with butter and dusting the insides with cocoa powder.
2. Preheat the oven to 160°C/325°F/gas mark 3.
3. Melt 250g (9 oz./1⅔ cups) of the chocolate chips together with the butter in a microwave or over a saucepan of simmering water.
4. Stir the ground coffee into the melted chocolate mixture (this makes the chocolate flavour more intense).

5. Add the sugar and stir thoroughly.
6. Add the flour and stir until incorporated. Although this does not seem like much flour, it is the ratio of ingredients that gives the brownie a gooey texture.
7. Stir in the beaten eggs.
8. Finally, fold in the remaining chocolate chips.
9. Pour the batter into the prepared tin and bake for 30 minutes.
10. Leave to cool completely and then turn out of the tin.

NOTES ON RECIPES:
Use medium-size eggs and, where possible, free range.

All oven temperatures vary slightly, so you may need to adjust the baking times by a few minutes more or a few minutes less.

CHOCOLATE CUPCAKES

for poop cupcakes

YOU WILL NEED

75g (2⅔ oz./⅓ cup)
unsalted butter, softened

125g (4½ oz./⅔ cup)
caster (superfine) sugar

2 eggs

175ml (6 fl. oz./¾ cup) milk

100g (3½ oz./¾ cup)
self-raising (self-rising) flour, sifted

1 tsp baking powder

1 tsp instant coffee granules

70g (2½ oz./¾ cup) cocoa powder,
unsweetened

1. Line a cupcake tin with paper cases.
2. Preheat the oven to 160°C/325°F/
gas mark 3.
3. Beat the butter and sugar together
in a mixer until pale and smooth.
4. Add the eggs and mix again.
5. Scrape down the sides of the
bowl, add the milk, then mix again.
6. Add the flour, baking powder,
coffee granules and cocoa powder
before beating the mixture for the
final time, ensuring it is all combined.
7. Using an ice-cream scoop or
spoons, drop the batter into the
cases and bake for 20–25 minutes.

VANILLA BUTTERCREAM

YOU WILL NEED

400g (14 oz./1¾ cups)
unsalted butter, softened

900g (2 lb./7⅔ cups) icing
(confectioner's) sugar, sifted

6–8 tbsp milk

½ tsp vanilla extract

1. Using an electric mixer, beat the
butter for 2–3 minutes or until it
is pale and fluffy. (If you are adding
Nutella or peanut butter – see below
– beat it in with the butter now.)
2. Scrape the sides of the bowl with a
spatula. Add half of the icing sugar and
mix again, starting slowly and building
up the speed, for 2–3 minutes.
3. Add the remaining icing sugar and
mix again for another 2–3 minutes.
4. Add the milk and vanilla extract and
mix again, starting slowly and building
up the speed, until the buttercream
is smooth, light, and fluffy.

For extra flavour, add any of the
following to the basic buttercream:
• 200g (7 oz.) Nutella (omit vanilla)
• 140g (5 oz.) peanut butter (omit vanilla)
• 200ml (7 fl. oz.) caramel sauce
• 200g (7 oz.) Maltesers, crushed

CHOCOLATE BUTTERCREAM

YOU WILL NEED

300g (10½ oz./1⅓ cups)
unsalted butter, softened

550g (19⅓ oz./4¾ cups)
icing (confectioner's) sugar

3–4 tbsp milk

200g (7 oz./1⅓ cups) dark chocolate
chips, melted and cooled

1. Using an electric mixer, beat the
butter for 2–3 minutes or until it is
pale and fluffy.
2. Scrape the sides of the bowl with a
spatula. Add half of the icing sugar and
mix again, starting slowly and building
up the speed, for 2–3 minutes.
3. Add the remaining icing sugar and
mix again for another 2–3 minutes.
4. Add the milk and mix again for
another 2–3 minutes.
5. Add the melted but not hot
chocolate and mix again, starting
slowly and building up the speed, until
the chocolate is fully incorporated
and the buttercream is smooth, light,
and fluffy.

• For an a.ternative flavour, replace
the dark chocolate with 200g (7 oz./
1⅓ cups) melted white chocclate.

CAKE FILLINGS

These cake recipes are simple and tasty, but you can also have fun with your fillings. Here are some ideas:

• Add peanut butter to the basic buttercream recipe and layer with caramel or raspberry jam.

• Add a mashed banana and ½ tsp ground cinnamon to the 15cm (6 in.) vanilla cake (double for 20cm or 8 in. cake) then layer with vanilla buttercream and caramel for a banoffee cake.

• Replace the vanilla from the 15cm (6 in.) cake with the zest of 1 unwaxed lemon (2 for 20cm or 8 in. cake) then layer with a good quality lemon curd.

• Put some marshmallows on a baking tray lined with parchment. Pop under a hot grill until they are browned (be careful they don't burn!) Whilst still warm, add them to the basic buttercream and beat on high speed for a toasted marshmallow buttercream which goes perfectly with the chocolate cake.

COOKIE DOUGH

for funfetti hearts and iced cookies

200g (7 oz./1½ cups) plain (all-purpose) flour, sifted

Pinch of salt

50g (1¾ oz./½ cup) ground almonds

75g (2⅔ oz./6 tbsp) caster (granulated) sugar

100g (3½ oz./½ cup) unsalted butter, softened

3 egg yolks

1 tsp vanilla extract

1. Line a baking tray with parchment.
2. Preheat the oven to 175°C/350°F/ gas mark 4.
3. Place the flour and salt into a mixing bowl. Add the ground almonds and caster (granulated) sugar and stir to combine.
4. Add the butter and mix at a slow speed until the mixture is crumbly and looks like sand.
5. Add the egg yolks and vanilla extract and mix again until a firm dough forms. Do not overmix.
6. Wrap the dough in plastic wrap and place in the fridge for at least 1 hour, preferably overnight.

7. Remove the dough from the fridge and knead to make it pliable. Roll out the dough on a floured surface to a thickness of 5mm (⅛ in.), using spacers to ensure an even thickness.
8. Cut out your cookie shapes (see pages 78–79) and put them on the prepared baking tray.
9. Put your cut-out cookies back into the fridge to chill before baking – this helps them keep their shape.
10. Bake the cookies for 10-12 minutes or until they are light golden brown on the top and sides. Check after 10 minutes, then if they are not ready, bake for a further 2 minutes before checking again.
11. Once baked, carefully transfer the cookies onto a wire rack to cool. They will still be soft when hot but will firm up as they cool.

LAYERING CAKES

1. Using a cake leveller or serrated knife, trim off the top of each sponge. For middle layers, trim off the base too. Make all layers the same depth.

2. If using a non-slip turntable, place the cake disc (or use an upside down cake tin) in the centre. Using buttercream or ganache, stick a cake board in the centre of the cake disc.

3. Using a palette knife, spread the board with a thin layer of buttercream or ganache. Stick the first sponge layer on the board.

4. Using a palette knife, spread your filling evenly over the first sponge layer, take it right to the edges. If using, spread a thin layer of jam on the underside of the next sponge layer. Place this sponge layer on top of the first with the jam side down.

5. Repeat steps 3 and 4 for any further middle layers until just the top layer is left. Place the final sponge layer on top and check that the cake is level.

CRUMB-COATING CAKES

1. Using a palette knife, spread any buttercream that has oozed out of the layers around the sides of the cake If necessary, spread more buttercream evenly around with the palette knife in a backwards and forwards motion.

2. Once the sides are covered, place a generous amount of buttercream on the top of the cake. Working from the centre, spread it out to the edges.

3. Make sure that the cake is entirely covered by the buttercream, with no gaps around the sides or on the top.

4. Hold a scraper against the side of the cake at a 45 degree angle and with the bottom of the scraper resting on the cake disc. Rotate the turntable.

5. Repeat the side scraping process until the coating is smooth with no gaps. Using a palette knife and side scraper, remove any excess frosting.

COLOURING BUTTERCREAM

TIP:
When adding colour to buttercream or fondant, always use a clean toothpick. Even when adding more. You do not want to contaminate your paste colour with either buttercream or fondant.

1. Using a palette knife, take a scoop of buttercream and place it on your board. Then using a toothpick, take a tiny amount of colour and place it on the board next to the buttercream.

2. Using the palette knife, gradually work together the scoop of buttercream and the paste colour.

3. Keep working the buttercream and colour together until they are fully blended and the colour is evenly distributed with no marbling.

4. Add the scoop of coloured buttercream to the bowl of uncoloured buttercream. Using a palette knife, work the coloured buttercream through.

5. Keep working until the buttercreams together until they are fully blended and the colour is evenly distrubuted with no marbling.

COLOURING FONDANT

1. Weigh out and knead the amount of fondant needed on a clean work surface until soft and pliable. Separate out an amount of the kneaded fondant into a small ball or sausage.

2. Using the tip of a toothpick, take a tiny amount of paste colour and spread it across the small ball or sausage of fondant. Fold over the fondant to cover the coloured spot.

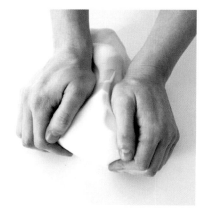

3. Knead the fondant until the colour is evenly distributed and no marbling remains. Keep adding tiny amounts of colour – blending different shades if necessary – until the exact shade.

4. To colour a large quantity of fondant, take a small piece of fully coloured fondant and add that to the larger piece.

5. Knead until the colour is evenly distributed throughout the fondant with no marbling. If the fondant sticks, use a little white vegetable fat on the surface.

COVERING A CAKE WITH FONDANT

1. On a surface lightly dusted with icing sugar, roll out the fondant to 3mm (⅛ in.) thickness using spacers to ensure an even thickness.

2. While rolling out the fondant, keep turning it 90 degrees in between each roll to ensure the fondant remains in a circular shape.

3. Using a cake smoother, work over the rolled-out fondant to smooth the surface and remove any wrinkles.

4. Using the rolling pin, lift the rolled-out fondant. Take care not to tear or stretch the fondant.

5. Place the rolled-out fondant over the cake, making sure that it is centred and the fondant is large enough to cover the sides of the cake.

6. Using a cake smoother, work over the top of the cake to remove any air pockets.

7. Using the palms of your hands, work the fondant down the sides of the cake.

TIPS:
If any air bubbles appear in the fondant, use a clean sterilised pin to prick them out and then smooth over the surface either with your hands or a cake smoother.

Try to work quickly so that the fondant doesn't dry out and crack. If any cracks or wrinkles do appear, they can be polished using another small lump of fondant.

8. Using a palette knife, trim around the base of the cake to remove the excess fondant.

9. Using cake smoothers, work over the top and sides of the covered cake to make sure that the surface is perfectly smooth.

ROLLING OUT COOKIE DOUGH

1. On a dusted surface roll out the dough to 5mm (⅝ in) thickness using spacers to ensure even thickness. Any thinner and the cookies may crack whilst baking.

2. Using a cookie cutter, punch out your cookie shapes.

3. Alternatively, make card templates for the different cookie shapes (see pages 94–95) and, using a sharp knife, cut carefully around the template outline to create the cookie shape.

4. Using a palette knife, transfer the cookie shapes onto a baking tray lined with parchment. Place the tray of cookies in the fridge for 30 minutes, then bake from chilled to prevent them from spreading.

CHOCOLATE GANACHE

makes 400g (14 oz.)

YOU WILL NEED

150g (5½ oz./1 cup) plain Belgian chocolate chips (minimum 53% cocoa solids)

100ml (3½ fl. oz./½ cup) whipping (heavy) cream

15g (½ oz./1 tbsp) glucose syrup

1. Place the chocolate drops in a large bowl. Pour the cream into a saucepan and add the glucose.

2. Bring the cream and glucose mixture to a simmer and then pour over the chocolate. Shake the bowl to evenly distribute the cream, then leave to sit for 1 minute.

3. Gently whisk until the chocolate has melted and the mixture is smooth and glossy.

4. Leave to cool before using. If covered with plastic wrap and stored in an airtight container, the ganache will keep for up to 2 weeks.

ROYAL ICING

makes 1kg (35 oz.)

--- YOU WILL NEED ---

1kg (35 oz./8½ cups) sifted icing (confectioners') sugar

Squeeze of lemon juice (optional)

6 medium (165g/6 oz.) egg whites

TIP:
You may want to cover the mixing bowl with a cloth to prevent the icing sugar from billowing everywhere when mixing.

1. Place all the icing sugar, lemon juice (if using) and three-quarters of the egg white into a large bowl or the bowl of an electric stand mixer fitted with the paddle attachment.

2. Mix by hand or on the slowest speed for about 5 minutes, until all the powdery sugar has disappeared and the mixture looks smooth, but not wet. If the mixture looks too dry, add more egg white.

3. Scrape down the sides of the bowl to make sure the icing sugar s combined. If the mixture is dry, add a little more liquid; if the mixture is runny, add a little more icing sugar.

4. Beat slowly for a further 4–5 minutes to remove any lumps and achieve an icing that has a smooth, satin-like texture and forms stiff peaks that hold their shape.

COLOURING ROYAL ICING

1. Take a small amount of stiff-peak icing and place it on a board. Using a toothpick, place a small amount of gel paste food colouring next to the icing on the board.

2. Using a palette knife, blend the food colouring with the stiff-peak icing. Keep working the icing until the colour is completely blended and there are no tiny specks of colour left.

TIP:
When colouring royal icing, always colour it at the stiff-peak stage and then loosen the coloured icing down to either soft-peak or flooding consistency. Adding colouring to a runnier consistency icing might thin it out too much.

3. Once blended, gradually add the coloured icing to a larger amount of white icing and mix together to achieve the required shade.

4. To loosen stiff-peak icing down to soft-peak icing add a small amount of water. Soft-peak icing is the perfect consistency when it looks glossy and forms soft peaks that slowly fall over.

FLOODING ROYAL ICING

There are three different consistencies of royal icing used throughout cake decorating — stiff peak, soft peak, and flooding or runny.

Stiff peak: this icing is a stiff paste that makes a peak and holds its shape when you lift a spoon from the mixture. Stiff peak icing is used to stick cakes to cards or drums and stick cake tiers together.

Soft peak: this icing is looser than stiff peak — it should still hold a peak, but the peak flops slightly. When gentle pressure is applied, soft peak icing runs freely from a piping bag. A piped line of soft peak icing holds its shape and is used to pipe the outline of cookies.

Flooding: this is the runniest consistency of icing that is used to fill in, or 'flood', the outlines on a cookie to create coloured sections. It shouldn't be so runny that is leaks from the piping bag, but when piped its surface should settle flat after around 10 seconds.

1. Transfer the coloured stiff-peak or soft-peak icing into a small bowl. Mix with a spatula and gradually add a little water until the icing looks shiny, flows, and flattens within 10 seconds.

2. To test the consistency, drag a palette knife through the icing about a few centimetres (an inch) deep. If the surface of the icing smooths over and returns to flat in 10 seconds then your icing is perfect flooding consistency.

3. Tap the bowl onto a hard surface to bring any air bubbles to the top and prick them with a toothpick, before placing the icing into a piping bag using a palette knife.

MAKING PIPING BAGS

TIP:
For extra strength, use waxed greaseproof paper, which is also called silicon paper, that can be bought from specialist baking suppliers. Alternatively, you can buy paper piping bags readymade from cake decorating suppliers.

1. Take a 35cm (14 in.) by 35cm (14 in.) square of greaseproof paper. Using scissors, cut diagonally from a corner to the one opposite, sliding the blades through the paper, to make a triangle.

2. Hold the triangle with the longest side furthest away from you and point closest to you. To form a cone, curl the right corner up and over to the top corner pointing towards you.

3. Wrap the left corner around the cone to join the other corners at the back of the cone. Slide the paper between your thumbs and fingers until the cone forms a sharp tip.

4. At the back of the cone, fold the corners over to the inside of the open end of the cone to prevent the piping bag from unravelling.

5. Snip off the tip of the piping bag before inserting a piping nozzle.

PIPING TECHNIQUES

TIP:
When not using, store any piping bags filled with icing in re-sealable plastic bags.

1. If using a nozzle, place it in the piping bag. Using a palette knife, transfer the icing into the bag. Only ever half-fill a piping bag otherwise the icing will ooze out when squeezed.

2. Flatten the open end of the piping bag and, with the seam centred on one side, fold over the ends of the bag away from the seam to keep the bag closed tight.

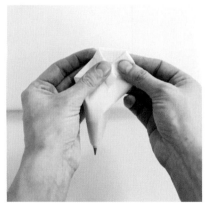

3. Fold in the two outside corners, then fold over the top of the bag. Continue folding until you cannot fold any more. This creates the pressure needed to make piping easier.

4. With the piping bag in your preferred hand, hold it between your thumb and fingers. Place your thumb over the folded end of the bag. Place your index finger down the seam.

5. Guiding the tip with your free hand, pipe the lines. Hold the bag at a 45° angle to the surface. Touch the starting point with the tip and squeeze out the icing. Lift 2.5cm (1 in.) and guide the line.

TEMPLATE FOR CRYING-LAUGHING FACE CAKE ON PAGES 6–9

**TEMPLATES FOR KISSY FACE AND
COOL DUDE FACE CAKES ON PAGES 6–9**

to enlarge photocopy at 200%

TEMPLATE FOR CAT CAKE
ON PAGES 18–21

TEMPLATE FOR GHOST CAKE ON PAGES 22–5

to enlarge photocopy at 200%

**TEMPLATE FOR
POOP CUPCAKES
ON PAGES 26–9**

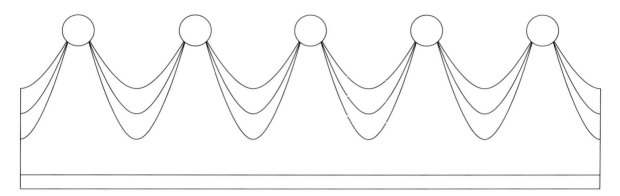

TEMPLATE FOR CROWN MINI CAKES ON PAGES 52–5

to enlarge photocopy at 200%

TEMPLATES FOR THREE WISE MONKEYS MINI CAKES ON PAGES 48–51

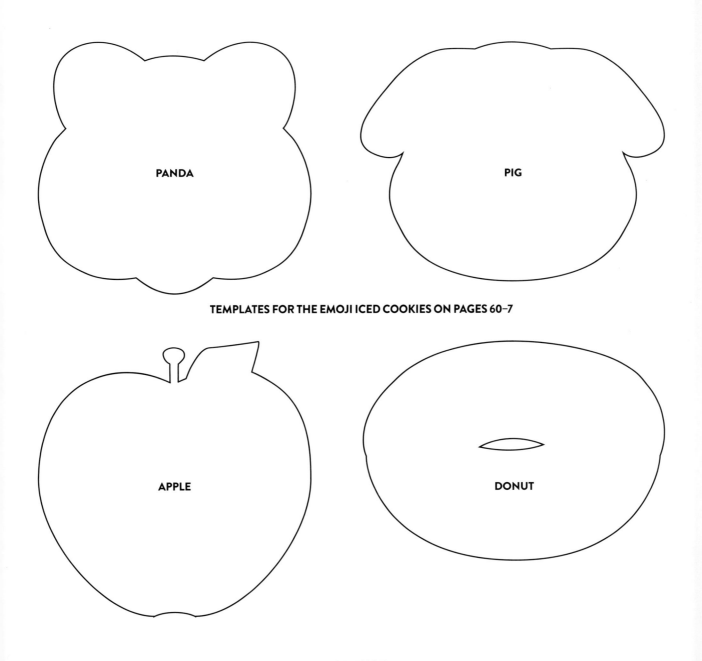

PANDA

PIG

TEMPLATES FOR THE EMOJI ICED COOKIES ON PAGES 60–7

APPLE

DONUT

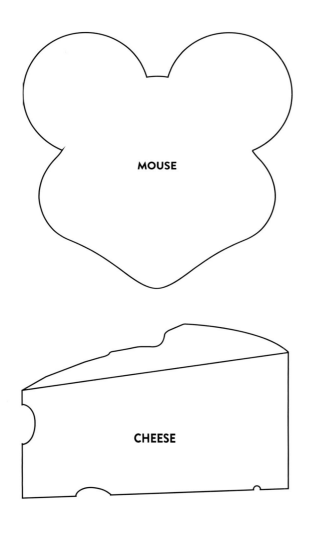

MOUSE

CAT

CHEESE

ICE CREAM

SHARE YOUR EMOJI BAKES ONLINE. POST YOUR PHOTOS WITH #CAKEMOJI

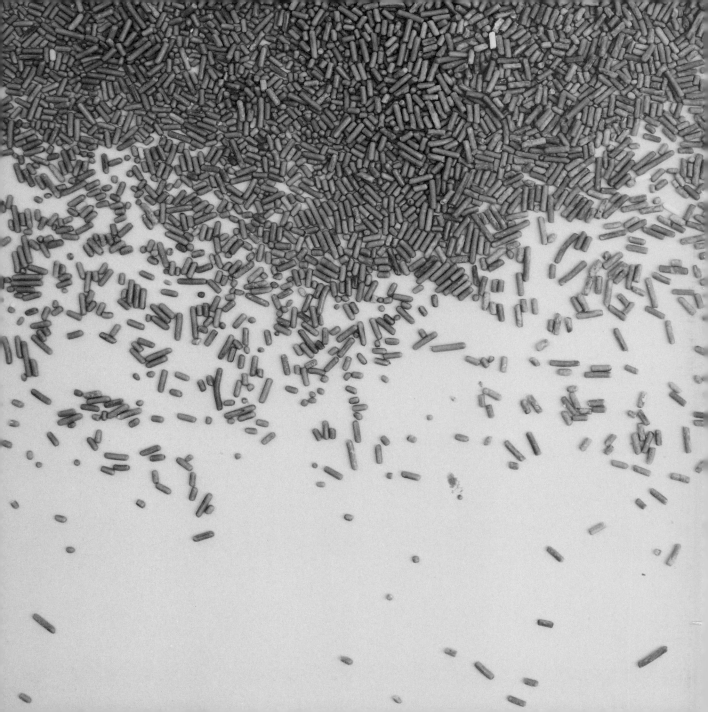